Piano • Vocal • Guitar

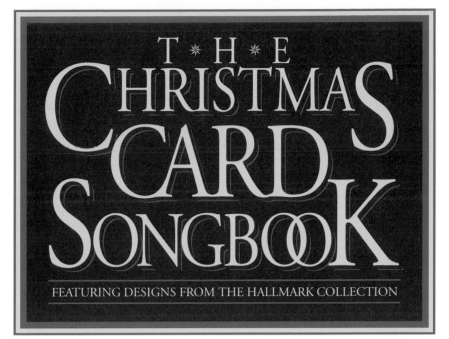

FEATURING DESIGNS FROM THE HALLMARK COLLECTION

From the Hallmark Historical Collection. This is a reproduction of an early twentieth century postcard designed by Ellen Clapsaddle, and originally printed in Germany for the International Art Publishing Company.

Hal Leonard Publishing Corporation

7777 West Bluemound Road
P.O.Box 13819 Milwaukee, Wisconsin 53213

Published by HAL LEONARD PUBLISHING CORPORATION
P.O. Box 13819, 7777 W. Bluemound Rd.
Milwaukee, WI 53213 USA

Printed in Hong Kong

CONTENTS

MERRY CHRISTMAS!

PREFACE

Christmas carols and cards are two of the most beloved traditions associated with the world's favorite holiday. Over the centuries, hundreds of artists and composers have been inspired by the Yuletide season, creating timeless classics in art and music that live on year after year. It seems only natural that these two elements should be combined to create THE CHRISTMAS CARD SONGBOOK.

With the generous help of the staff at Hallmark Cards, we are pleased to offer THE CHRISTMAS CARD SONGBOOK featuring selections from the virtually endless array of Hallmark designs to help everyone understand, appreciate and celebrate the Christmas season. To you and yours, for this Christmas season and in all those yet to come, Noël!

THE STORY OF THE CHRISTMAS CARD

The joy of sending and receiving Christmas cards has a colorful history dating to the days of the stage coach and penny postage, according to the folks at Hallmark Cards, Inc.

More than a century ago, in 1843, London businessman Henry Cole originated the Christmas card custom. His idea of Christmas in an envelope came only three years after the English postal reform that made it possible to send mail to friends near and far for a penny.

Cole asked an artist friend, John Calcott Horsley of the Royal Academy, to design the card in 1843, when Cole didn't have time to write the customary personal messages. The card was divided into three panels, with the main illustration showing the elders at a friendly family party raising wine glasses in a toast. The panels on either side showed two of the oldest traditions of Christmas – feeding the hungry and clothing the needy. "A Merry Christmas and A Happy New Year To You," still the most popular holiday sentiment, was the message.

Original prints of the card are both rare and valuable. Only a dozen are known to exist, including two in the 40,000-card Hallmark Historical Collection, the largest collection of antique and historical cards in the world.

Greeting card firms began springing up in England during the 1860s. England's best known woman artist and illustrator of children's books, Kate Greenaway, designed greeting cards for Marcus Ward and Co. of London.

Popular Christmas card designs of the 1860s and '70s included few religious scenes. The most popular designs were landscapes, children, flowers, portraits, birds, animals and fish.

Louis Prang of Boston perfected in the 1870s the lithographic process of multicolor printing, often using as many as 20 colors on one card. His reproductions of oil paintings were so accurate that at times only experts could tell print from painting.

Hallmark Product Archives, Hallmark Cards, Inc.

By 1881 Prang was printing 5 million cards a year, most of them Christmas cards. He sponsored art contests to get card design, with prizes as high as $1,000.

Near the turn of the century, penny postcards made in Germany flooded the market. Rather than compromise the quality of his cards, Prang discontinued their manufacture in 1895. From then until World War I, Germany monopolized the postcard trade.

Most of today's major greeting card publishers emerged about 1910, and by 1920 were meeting the public demand for cards of better quality and design.

In 1929, the Depression hit. Cards of the period often spoofed poverty and expressed faith that better times were ahead.

The industry survived the Depression only to run head-on into World War II. Santa and Uncle Sam carrying flags became popular designs. Special cards came out for servicemen. "Across The Miles" and "Missing You" sentiments reflected the reality of the day.

The Cold War years sharpened a demand for more humor in Christmas cards. This sparked the studio card, with its funny Santas and silly reindeer.

Hallmark Product Archives, Hallmark Cards, Inc.

Hallmark Product Archives, Hallmark Cards, Inc.

Hallmark Product Archives,
Hallmark Cards, Inc.

9

Hallmark Product Archives, Hallmark Cards, Inc.

Flower children, peace symbols and designs celebrating the first manned moon landing came into vogue during the 1960s and '70s. In the early 1980s, cards depicted the fitness craze, showing Santa outfitted in jogging suit and running shoes, and participating in sports. Other cards captured the '80s by spoofing TV shows and commercials.

Today's trends in Christmas cards show a renewed interest in traditional designs (trees, wreaths, red and green, home settings) that are both colorful and elegant. Religious cards remain popular, and many of them are contemporary, using bright graphics with short, upbeat prose sentiments.

The Christmas card-sending custom has weathered war, economic turmoil and vast social changes for more than a century. It serves a timeless human need to stay close, to share special thoughts and feelings with friends far and near during our most cherished holiday season.

Each year it is estimated that 2.2 billion Christmas cards are given.

Hallmark Product Archives, Hallmark Cards, Inc.

Hallmark Product Archives, Hallmark Cards, Inc.

Hallmark Product Archives, Hallmark Cards, Inc.

THE SYMBOLS OF CHRISTMAS AS REFLECTED ON CHRISTMAS CARDS

Christmas cards aren't always what they appear to be.

Ever since the first-known commercially printed Christmas greeting was designed in 1843 in London, critics have complained about the lack of attention to the religious aspect of the holiday.

Very often the religious symbolism is there, but unrecognized by the layman.

Even the first card, which was criticized by temperance groups because it pictured a family with wine glasses raised in a toast, was full of symbolism. Artist John Calcott Horsley, who designed the card for London businessman Henry Cole, made good use of the religious symbolism of Christmas. His side panels depicted the virtues of feeding the poor and clothing the naked. But more than that, Horsley wound sprigs of holly, the symbol of chastity, and ivy, symbolic of where God had walked, through the design.

In the Hallmark Historical Collection, largest and most representative of early greeting card art in the world, one can see such design elements as evergreens, birds, animals and musical instruments used to symbolize the rich traditions and legends of Christmas.

One of the most popular images used by the early designers was the robin. According to legend, a small brown bird fanned the embers of a dying fire in the manger one night to keep the Christ Child warm. As the flames leapt from the coals, the little bird's breast was seared scarlet, but he kept at his chore. Today, artists use the robin red breast to symbolize courage and charity.

Flying birds frequently symbolize spiritual life and a peacock in a design stands for eternal life. And, of course, the dove traditionally has been the sign of peace.

© Hallmark Cards, Inc.

11

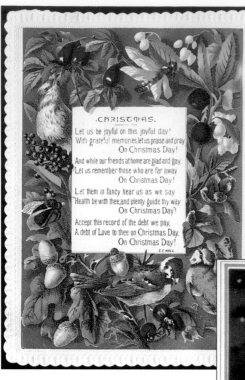

Lambs symbolize Christ, who was the Lamb of God, and call attention to his later sacrifice on the cross, while sheep are used to indicate that all living things owe allegiance to their Creator. Such beasts of burden as oxen and donkeys often symbolize humility.

Many of the legends from which artists have borrowed ideas revolve around trees and flowers.

The white rose that appears on many Christmas cards comes from the tale of the little shepherd girl who broke into tears as she walked to the manger because she had no gift for the Christ Child. An angel, seeing her plight, turned her tears into white roses with which to decorate the manger.

The poinsettia had a similar beginning. In a Mexican folk tale, a peasant boy who had no money for a gift gathered simple greenery along the road to Bethlehem. But before he arrived at the manger, an angel appeared and turned the green leaves to scarlet flowers.

Nothing plays a more symbolic part in the art of Christmas than the evergreen, which is the subject of many legends.

According to one, on the night Christ was born, all the trees in the forest burst into bloom in honor of the birth, and have continued to bear fruit year round ever since.

The legend of the pine tree tells us that the pine was once mortal. Like other trees, it was green in summer, bare and brown in winter.

One giant pine tree, its branches brittle and half its trunk hollowed out by disease, stood by a road in Israel where Joseph and Mary passed as they fled with the Christ Child from the soldiers of King Herod. Joseph led Mary and the Child into the hollow trunk to rest and hide. The pine tree, full of pity, dropped its protective branches down to cover them while Herod's troops rode by. All night it hid them. The next morning, the Child awoke and blessed the pine tree and pronounced that forevermore its branches would be green both summer and winter.

The Germans have provided us with one of the more delightful folk tales about the origin of the Christmas tree. According to the legend, just as a woodsman and his family were about to retire on Christmas Eve, there was a knock on the door. It was a small child, shivering with cold and hunger. The family took the child in, fed him, and gave him a place to sleep.

The next morning the family was awakened by a choir of angels caroling in the sky. To their joy and amazement, they discovered that it was the Christ Child whom they had entertained. He stood before them transfigured, and before he disappeared, he took a twig from a fir tree, planted it in the ground and said: "I have gladly received your gifts, and here is mine to you; this tree will never fail to bear its fruit at Christmas and you shall always have abundance."

The use of an evergreen as a Christmas tree comes to us from Germany, and while Christmas trees are believed to have been introduced into this country by Hessian soldiers during the Revolutionary War, the custom came into its own only about 100 years ago.

Symbolic significance of the evergreen branches of the Christmas tree is tied closely to the Christian belief in everlasting life.

Martin Luther is frequently credited with originating the custom of decorating evergreen trees and bringing them into the house. And the decorations have their legends and symbolism, too.

The Glory of God is symbolized by Christmas lights and the red holly berries commonly used for decoration in earlier years symbolize the drops of blood caused by the crown of thorns.

The use of tinsel on Christmas trees springs from an old story about some little house spiders who spun their silk to decorate the bare tree of a poor but good German woman who had been kind to them. An angel, impressed by their charity, touched the tree and turned the spider webs to shining silver.

Mistletoe was first used by the British along with holly and ivy to decorate their somber halls. Since mistletoe was a key part of ancient Druid winter solstice rites, church authorities in England banned the bush from churches for a time. The custom of kissing under the mistletoe springs, by the way, from the Druid tradition of marrying under giant oak trees decorated with mistletoe.

© Hallmark Cards, Inc.

From The Hallmark Historical Collection.
From an original 1882 card published by Louis Prang & Co., Boston.

13

No story about Christmas cards would be complete without Santa Claus. And artists have portrayed Santa in a variety of ways.

Until Dr. Clement Clarke Moore wrote his classic poem, "A Visit from St. Nicholas" in 1822, and described Santa Claus as a right jolly old elf with a white beard and a little round belly, there was no accepted way that Santa was supposed to look.

Even then, it took another forty years before political cartoonist Thomas Nast, the man who created the elephant and donkey symbols for the two major political parties, popularized Moore's Santa in his drawings for magazines and newspapers.

Until that time, Santa took on whatever form the artist imagined.

Some Santas were thin and in some cases bore striking resemblance to popular leaders.

The most popular Santa of the old days, however, was the Father Christmas figure, a stately, bearded gentleman dressed in clerical robes.

Researchers at Hallmark say that "Santa Claus" is a distortion of "Saint Nicholas," who was brought to this country in the early 18th century by Dutch colonists. Saint Nicholas was difficult for children to pronounce, so the name was simplified in stages: first to "sinterklas," and finally to "Santa Claus."

The original Saint Nicholas is believed to have been a 4th century archbishop of Myra, a city in Turkey, who devoted his life to good deeds and gift-giving.

For many years in Europe, the gift-giving that we associate with Christmas took place on December 6, St. Nicholas Day, and even today in many Catholic countries, children receive gifts from St. Nicholas on December 6.

When the Protestant Reformation swept over Northern Europe, the reformers attempted to wipe out all veneration of saints. One of the targets was Saint Nicholas.

But the Protestants, or perhaps the children of the Protestants, borrowed a chapter from their Catholic predecessors. As the Catholics had "Christianized" certain pagan festivals, so did the Protestants "Protestantize" certain Catholic festivals.

As a result, Saint Nicholas began to pop up all over Europe at Christmas with a different name: Père Noël in France, Father Christmas in England, Kris Kringle in Germany.

Whatever he was called, and whenever he came, Santa Claus brought gifts to children. He loved them. And they loved him.

In Europe, Santa Claus traveled by popular conveyance – in many cases, horsedrawn cart.

The sleigh with its reindeer is a purely American invention with the first known reference appearing in 1821 in a publication called "The Children's Friend."

But it took time, even in America, for Santa to move exclusively to the sleigh. Some early greeting cards in the Hallmark Historical Collection show him arriving by other means. One shows Santa riding an antique bicycle.

Even though the facts point to the American Santa Claus being of Dutch origin, greeting cards as we know them today are a phenomenon of the English-speaking world. As a result, the Father Christmas figure was more often used on antique Christmas cards.

But Thomas Nast changed that when his drawings began appearing in the 1860s, and by the time that the modern era of greeting card publishing began, approximately 1910, Santa Claus as we know him today was firmly established.

Christmas cards have come a long way since 1843. Designs are more sophisticated. Production processes have been refined. But the message on that first Christmas card is as relevant today as it was then.

"A Merry Christmas and a Happy New Year to You."

From the Hallmark Fine Art Collection. Original artwork by Haddon Sundblom.

From the Hallmark Historical Collection. Reproduced from an original 1886 card published by Louis Prang, Boston; designed by Walter Satterlee.

Hallmark Product Archives, Hallmark Cards, Inc.

CHRISTMAS TRADITIONS AROUND THE WORLD

In other parts of the world you might find yourself celebrating Christmas by skiing down a mountain side with a lighted torch in your hand... strewing hay on the floor of your home... knocking on a neighbor's door in a symbolic pilgrimage.

In Poland, in memory of Christ's birth in a manger, families spread hay on the floor at their festive Christmas Eve meal; Lithuanians scatter straw under the tablecloth.

The colorful Mexican posada represents the drama of Mary's and Joseph's search for that manger. On each of the nine nights before Christmas, a couple dressed as Mary and Joseph go from house to house. Only at the last house are they and the neighbors parading behind them invited in for supper.

Even more novel is a procession in the mountains of Bavaria. Natives of Oberammergau gather on Christmas Eve to ski down the mountain slopes with flaming torches in their hands, singing as they go.

From The Hallmark Product Archives.

Every country celebrating Christmas has its own rituals. In Sweden the Christmas season begins on December 13 with the feast of St. Lucia. Each community chooses a lovely Lucia Queen as the young girl martyred for her religion centuries ago in ancient Rome.

In some countries gifts are given twice during the Christmas season. On Christmas Eve Italian children and their elders draw small gifts from a jar called the Urn of Fate, while waiting for their Santa Claus (Befana) to come on January 6. The French exchange gifts on New Year's Day but their Santa (Père Noël) visits youngsters on Christmas Eve too.

From The Hallmark Historical Collection. This design is a reproduction of a postcard published in Germany in 1915.

The British celebrate December 26 as Boxing Day, when servants and tradespeople are remembered with boxes of money.

Almost universally, Christmas is also a time for feasting and menus vary greatly. The French reveillon, a feast after midnight mass, often features oysters and sausages. In the French province of Brittany, buckwheat cakes with sour cream spice the meal. The Norwegian Christmas dinner includes a fish called leutefisk. In Poland Christmas dinner is served in seven, nine, or eleven courses. A Lithuanian Christmas feast has twelve courses, for the twelve disciples.

"Deck the Halls with boughs of holly" is a traditional refrain in English and American homes and holly has long been a part of the Christmas scene. In the Middle Ages it was thought to hold protective powers. A few hundred years ago maidens attached sprigs of it to their beds on Christmas Eve to protect them from evil during the coming year.

Mistletoe has an equally ancient and romantic background. Primitive Britons called it "all heal" and thought its magic powers could heal disease, neutralize poisons, confound witchcraft and assure fertility in humans and animals. They believed a young couple sealing their betrothal with a kiss under the mistletoe would have good luck the rest of their lives.

Thousands of years before Christ the evergreen stood for long life and immortality. German tribemen brought fir trees into their homes to cajole the god-like "spirits" they thought lived in the branches.

The Christmas tree so popular in the United States and Northern Europe is somewhat rare in Southern Europe, where the creche or manger scene appears more often.

Perhaps the most unusual Christmas tradition is observed by Swiss romantics. They tell a boy or girl to visit nine fountains and sip three times from each while the bells are ringing for midnight services on Christmas Eve. Afterwards, they'll find their future husband or wife standing at the door of the church, the beginning of a courtship if the spell has worked.

From the Hallmark Historical Collection. This is a reproduction of a postcard originally published in the early 1900s when postcards were a popular form of greeting.

© Hallmark
Cards, Inc.

A HISTORY OF THE CHRISTMAS CAROL

The oldest known Christmas song was written about 1600 years ago. St. Ambrose of Italy was probably the author of the late 4th century Latin carol, "Veni, Redemptor Gentium." In its English form, "Come, Thou Redeemer of the Earth," it is still sung today.

Up to about 1400, relatively few carols were created, and mainly in Latin and Greek. The components of the oldest well-known carol, "Veni, Emmanuel" ("O Come, O Come, Emmanuel") were probably written around the 12th century. However, it was not assembled as a carol until the mid-nineteenth century. If "O Come, O Come, Emmanuel" is not to be regarded as the earliest famous carol, then that honor would go to "La marche des rois" ("The March Of The Kings"), a vigorous 13th century folk phenomenon from Provence, France.

Hallmark Product Archives, Hallmark Cards, Inc.

Around 1400 in England, and somewhat earlier on the continent, two changes developed in the carol. First, vernacular or national languages steadily replaced Latin and Greek. Second, the carol evolved as a popular dance form. This new type of song was a reaction to the strictness and puritanism of the Middle Ages and the increased secularism and humanism of the blossoming Renaissance. The carol really began to flourish in the 15th century, producing enduring songs like "The Boar's Head Carol" and "Coventry Carol," both from England, and "Es ist ein' Ros' Entsprungen" ("Lo, How a Rose E'er Blooming") from Germany.

The 16th century was the greatest era for the carol. That fertile period probably produced "God Rest Ye Merry, Gentlemen," "The First Noel," "Tomorrow Shall Be My Dancing Day," "We Wish You A Merry Christmas," the dominant tune for "What Child Is This?," and the original tune for "While Shepherds Watched Their Flocks By Night" in England, "Deck The Hall" in Wales, and "O Tannenbaum" ("O Christmas Tree") and "Von Himmel hoch, da komm Ich her" ("From Heaven Above To Earth I Come") in Germany.

But in the 17th and 18th centuries, the carol suffered a decline. In fact, the secular celebration of Christmas was actually banned in England for a few years starting in 1644. Yet several fine carols were created in this lesser period. England was once again the land of carols, producing the folk songs "Here We Come A-Wassailing," "The Holly And The Ivy," and "The Twelve Days Of Christmas," plus the lyrics for "While Shepherds Watched Their Flocks by Night," "Joy To The World," and "Hark! The Herald Angels Sing." In addition, "Adeste Fideles" ("O Come All Ye Faithful") was created in France.

The carol bounced back strongly in the 19th century with a serious interest in collecting and printing old carols, plus the composition of a number of new songs. In Austria, the most popular carol, "Stille Nacht, Heilige Nacht" ("Silent Night, Holy Night") was written. In France "Cantique Noël" ("O Holy Night") was composed. In England "Angels from the Realms of Glory" was created, plus the lyrics for "What Child Is This?," "Good King Wenceslas" and "Good Christian Men Rejoice." In Germany, the tune for "Hark! The Herald Angels Sing" was composed.

Carol creation was actively pursued in the United States at the same time, primarily after mid-century. The music for "Joy To The World," the lyrics for "I Heard The Bells On Christmas Day," plus "It Came Upon the Midnight Clear," "We Three Kings Of Orient Are," "Jingle Bells," "O Little Town of Bethlehem," "Jolly Old St. Nicholas," and "Go Tell It On The Mountain," made the 19th century in America an exceptional era.

Numerous Christmas songs were conceived in the 20th century, but religious carols were few, especially after World War II. Building on the artistic promise of the late 19th century, the United States clearly became the leader. The most productive period was the 1930s, 1940s and 1950s. Those three decades brought us "Santa Claus Is Comin' To Town," "Winter Wonderland," "White Christmas," "The Christmas Song," "Rudolph the Red-nosed Reindeer," "Frosty The Snowman," "Silver Bells," and other popular favorites.

Since the 1950s, few good Christmas songs have been written. Perhaps the 1990s and the 21st century will bring a revival of carol production, including some significant religious tributes to the holidays.

© Hallmark Cards, Inc.

From The Hallmark Historical Collection. *This is a reproduction of a card from the Artistic Series published by Raphael Tuck & Sons, London, ca. 1883.*

May the Christmas Star that led, the Shepherds to the Manger bed Upon your heart shine soft and clear, and guide you through the dawning year.

From the Hallmark Historical Collection. In 1880, Louis Prang and Co. of Boston held the first of five Christmas card design competitions. This is a reproduction of that year's first prize design, "Christmas Music," by Rosina Emmett.

ALL MY HEART THIS NIGHT REJOICES

Paul Gerhardt, a Lutheran minister, was perhaps the most influential German hymn writer except for the great reformer Luther. This fine 1653 tribute to Christmas joy amazingly came from a soul deeply scarred by personal tragedy. The 1894 melody by Horatio Parker, Chair of Music at Yale University, is one of several used with the carol.

ALL MY HEART THIS NIGHT REJOICES

PAULUS GERHARDT, 1653
HORATIO PARKER, 1844
Translated by CATHERINE WINKWORTH

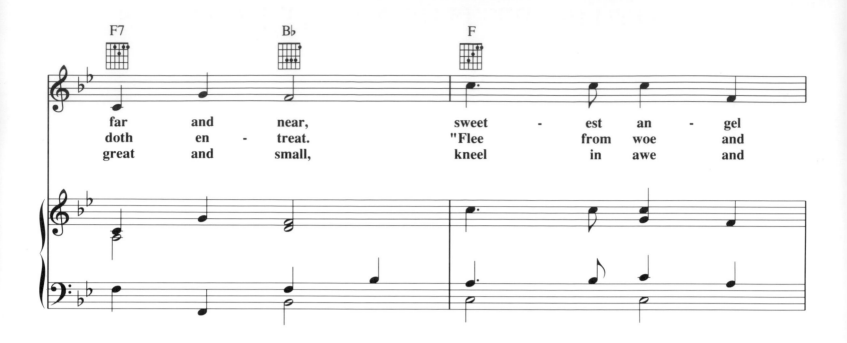

far and near,
sweet - est an - gel
doth en - treat.
"Flee from woe and
great and small,
kneel in awe and

voic - es.
dan - ger.
won - der.
"Christ is born,"
Breth - ren come who
Love Him with
their from

choirs are _____ sing - ing.
all that _____ grieves you
love is _____ yearn - ing.
Till the air,
You are the freed.
Hail the star,

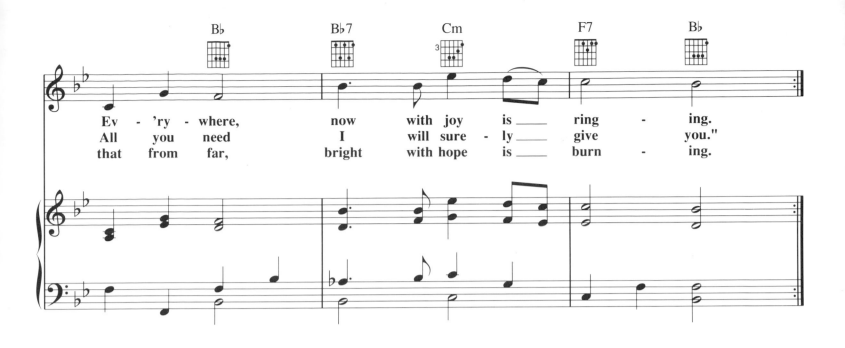

Ev - 'ry - where, now with joy is ____ ring - ing.
All you need I will sure - ly ____ give you."
that from far, bright with hope is ____ burn - ing.

ANGELS FROM THE REALMS OF GLORY

When English hymn writer, journalist, and social activist James Montgomery created the lyrics to this great carol in 1816, he based them on the fine 18th century French carol "Angels We Have Heard On High." At first the melody of the French song was used with Montgomery's words, but in time a better fitting 1867 tune by blind English composer Henry Smart generally displaced the earlier one.

ANGELS FROM THE REALMS OF GLORY

Words by JAMES MONTGOMERY
Music by HENRY SMART

ANGELS WE HAVE HEARD ON HIGH

Historical confusion muddles the background of this splendid carol and its most common English translation. Despite wild claims of second century origins and similar misinformation, the anonymous song is almost surely from 18th century France. The translation first appeared in England in 1862, but did not take its familiar form until a 1916 American carol collection.

ANGELS WE HAVE HEARD ON HIGH

French-English

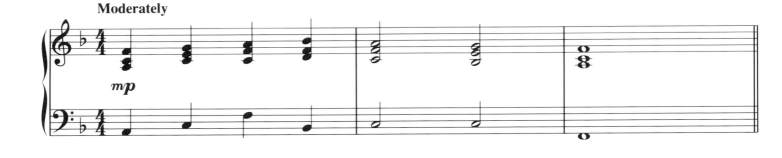

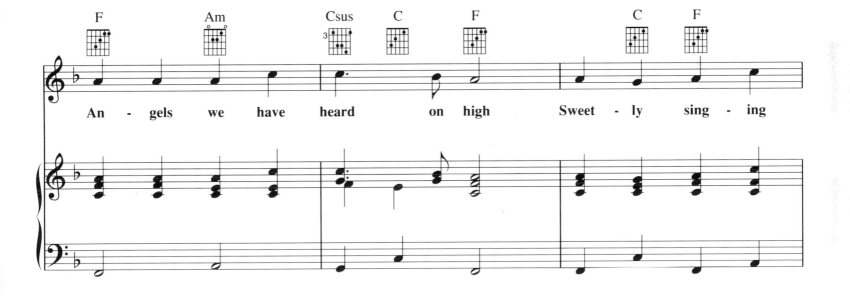

An - gels we have heard on high Sweet - ly sing - ing

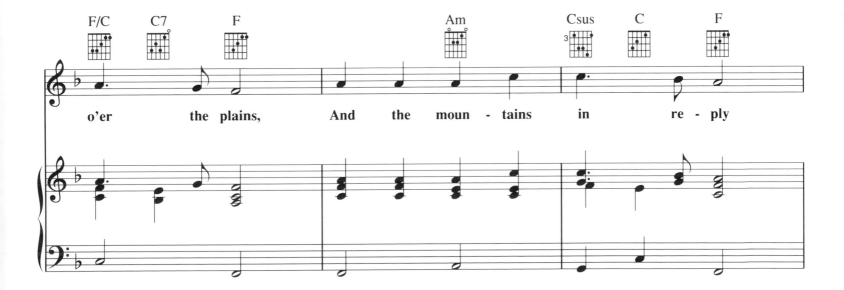

o'er the plains, And the moun - tains in re - ply

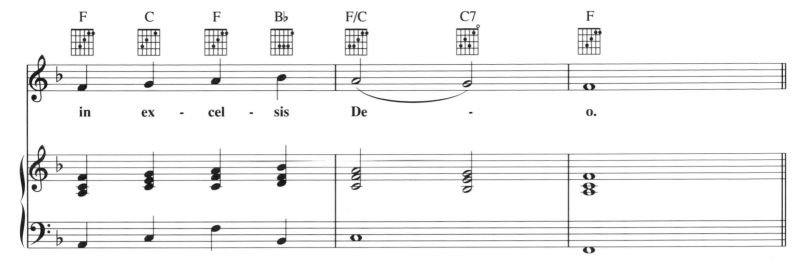

in ex - cel - sis De - o.

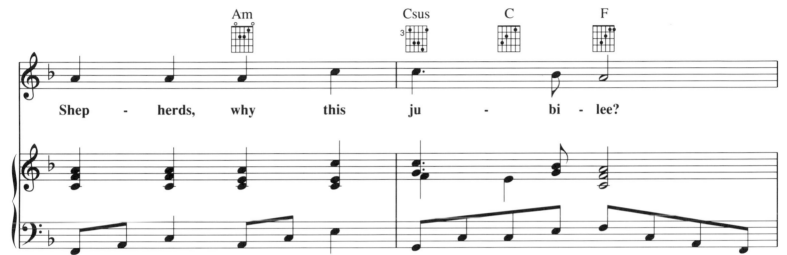

Shep - herds, why this ju - bi - lee?

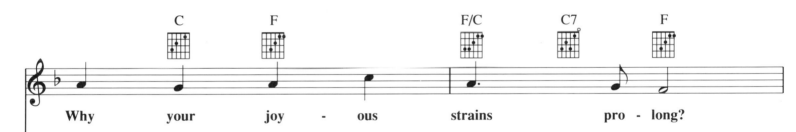

Why your joy - ous strains pro - long?

What the glad - some tid - ings be

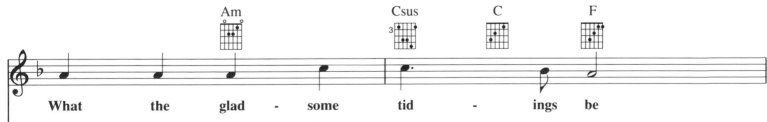

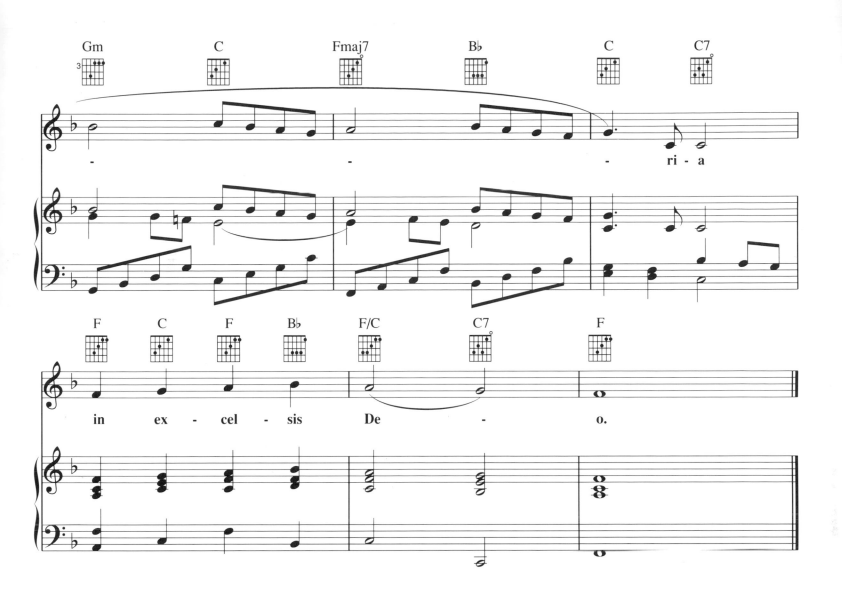

AWAY IN A MANGER (Murray)

No matter what you may have heard, Martin Luther was in no way associated with "Away In A Manger." The words were anonymous, and were first published in Philadelphia in 1885. The first (and most popular) melody connected with the lyrics was composed by American James Ramsey Murray in 1887. The "Carl Mueller" sometimes mentioned as composer of the tune appears to be totally imaginary.

AWAY IN A MANGER

Music by
JAMES R. MURRAY

AWAY IN A MANGER (Spilman)

There have been many variant melodies connected with this carol's anonymous words, which were first published in Philadelphia in 1885. The second most popular tune is the march-like setting written by American Jonathan E. Spilman in 1838. Spilman's melody was originally intended for the English folk ballad "Flow Gently Sweet Afton."

AWAY IN A MANGER

Music by
JONATHAN E. SPILMAN

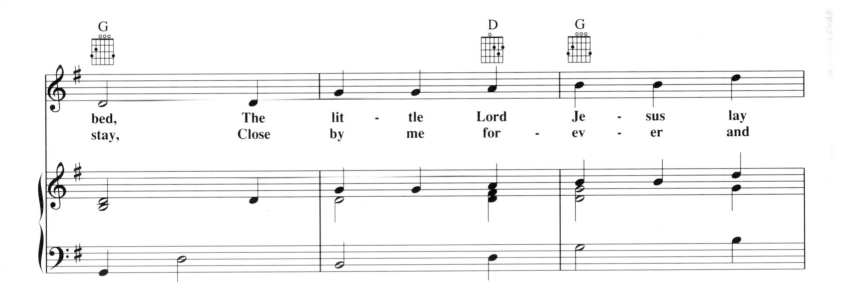

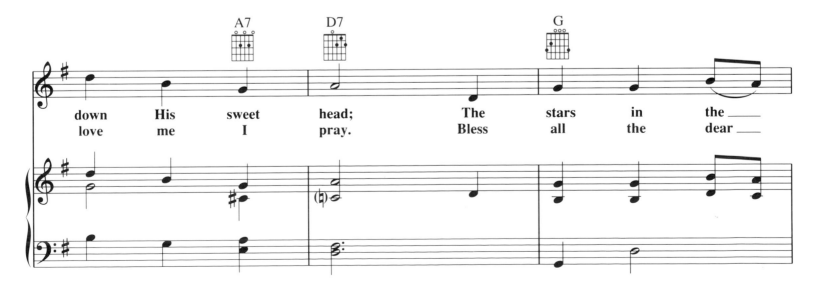

CAROL OF THE BELLS

The brilliant music for "Carol Of The Bells" has been made famous in recent years by its appearance in a series of champagne commericals. It was composed in 1916 by the Ukranian classical musician Mykola Dmytrovich Leontovych. The original form of the lyrics were by American Peter J. Wilhousky (1936), and this set of American words was anonymously published in 1972.

CAROL OF THE BELLS

MYKOLA D. LEONTOVYCH, 1916

Hark to the bells, hark to the bells, tell-ing us all Je-sus is King!

Strong-ly they chime, sound with a rhyme, Christ-mas is here! wel-come the King.

Hark to the bells, Hark to the bells, This is the day, day of the King!

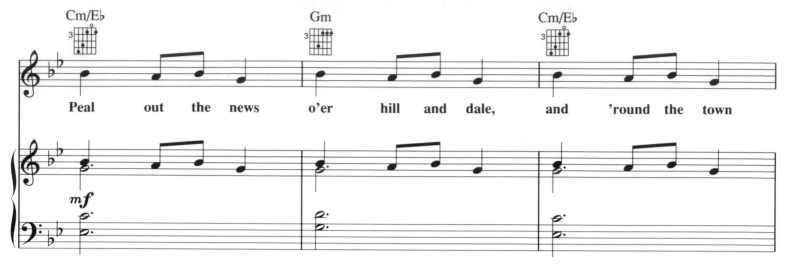

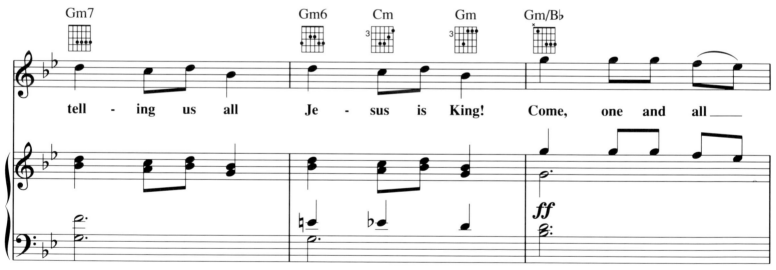

44

 HE CHRISTMAS SONG

It may seem a bit arrogant to call any song "The Christmas Song" as if there were no other pieces composed for the holiday. Yet this smooth, nostalgic popular masterpiece fits so well with the audacious claim of its title. Incidentally, Mel Torme and Robert Wells wrote this 1946 winter classic in the middle of a summer heat wave.

THE CHRISTMAS SONG

Music and Lyric by MEL TORME
and ROBERT WELLS

Chest - nuts roast - ing on an o - pen fire,
knows a tur - key and some mis - tle - toe

Jack Frost nip - ping at your nose,
help to make the sea - son bright.

Yule - tide car - ols be - ing
Ti - ny tots___ with their

sung by a choir and folks dressed up like Es - ki - mos. Ev -'ry -bod - y

eyes all a - glow will

find it hard to sleep to - night. They know that San - ta's on his

way; He's load - ed lots of toys and good - ies on his sleigh. And ev -'ry

moth - er's child_____ is gon - na spy_____ to see if

rein - deer ___ real - ly know how to fly. And
so, I'm of - fer - ing this sim - ple phrase to
kids from one to nine - ty two. Al - tho' it's been said man - y
times, man - y ways; "Mer - ry Christ - mas to you."

rit.

From the Hallmark Historical Collection. Postcards were at the height of their popularity when this design was originally published in 1908 by Julius Bien and Company of New York.

 HE CHRISTMAS WALTZ

As a songwriting team, lyricist Sammy Cahn and composer Jule Styne are best known for their collaboration on "Let It Snow! Let It Snow! Let It Snow!" (1945) and the Academy Award winning, "Three Coins In The Fountain" (1954). Less known is this attractive 1954 contribution to the holiday season.

THE CHRISTMAS WALTZ

Words by SAMMY CAHN
Music by JULE STYNE

DECK THE HALL

If any carol could be characterized as totally uninhibited, it would be this very merry tribute to holiday pleasure. The historical background on the song is fuzzy, but it appears that the compelling lyrics (originally probably in English) and the exceptional melody are both from Wales. The best guess as to dating it would be the 16th century.

DECK THE HALL

Welsh

Deck the hall with
See the blaz - ing
Fast a - way the

boughs of hol - ly, Fa la la la la, la la la la.
yule be - fore us, Fa la la la la, la la la la.
old year pass - es, Fa la la la la, la la la la.

'Tis the sea - son to be jol - ly, Fa la la la la, la
Strike the harp and join the cho - rus. Fa la la la la, la
Hail the new, ye lads and lass - es Fa la la la la, la

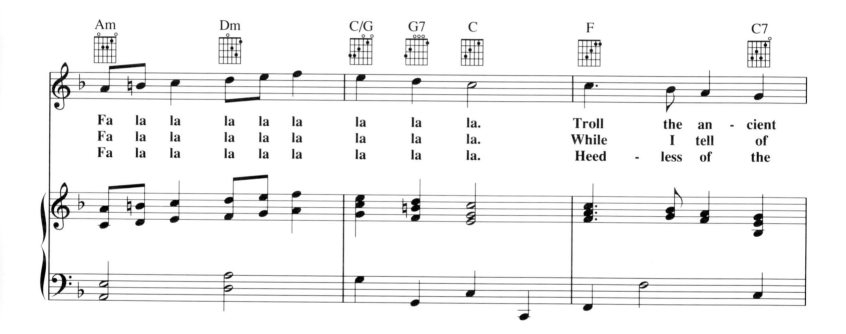

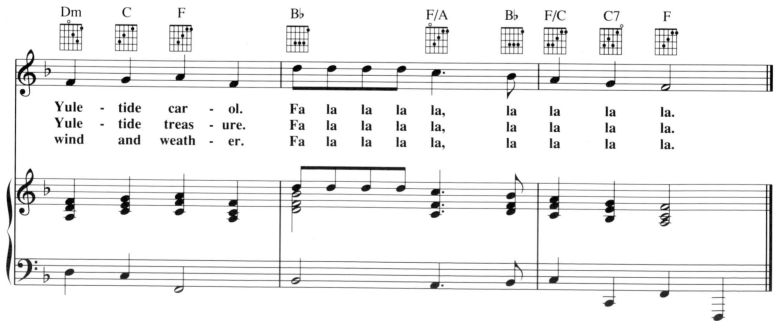

From the Hallmark Historical Collection. Reproduced from an original 1910 postcard published by International Art Publishing Co., Germany. Designed by Ellen Clapsaddle.

THE FIRST NOEL

In spite of the common use of the word "Noel" with this folk carol, the song is not French in origin, but is instead completely English. More properly called "The First Nowell," it is a product of 16th century Cornwall, a remote southwestern region of England. Although the lyrics are not particularly good, the enduring melody makes the carol among the most popular pieces from Britain.

THE FIRST NOEL

they lay__ keep - ing their sheep, On a cold win - ter's night __ that

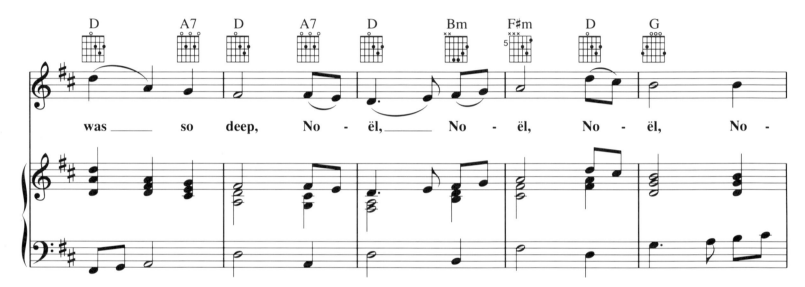

was _____ so deep, No - ël, _____ No - ël, No - ël, No -

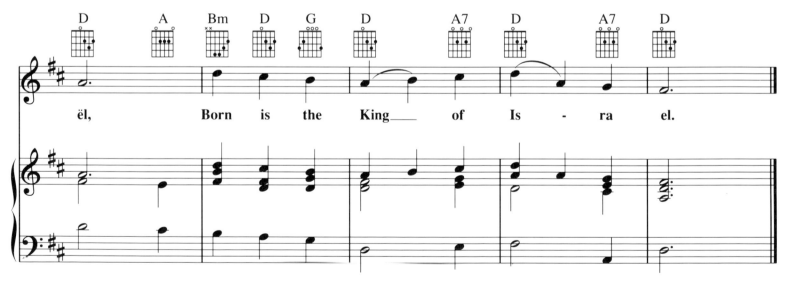

ël, Born is the King__ of Is - ra el.

Additional Lyrics

2. They looked up and saw a star
   Shining in the East, beyond them far;
   And to the earth it gave great light,
   And so it continued both day and night.

3. And by the light of that same star,
   Three wise men came from country far;
   To seek for a King was their intent,
   And to follow the star wherever it went.

4. This star drew night to the northwest,
   O'er Bethlehem it took its rest;
   And there it did both stop and stay,
   Right over the place where Jesus lay.

5. Then entered in those wise men three,
   Full reverently upon their knee;
   And offered there in His presence,
   Their gold, and myrrh, and frankincense.

FROM HEAVEN ABOVE TO EARTH I COME

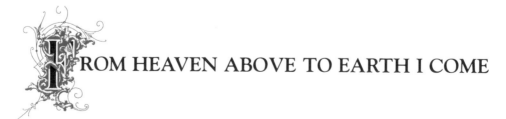

Martin Luther reportedly wrote the 1535 lyrics as part of a Christmas Eve
ceremony for his son Hans. Four years later, he composed the famous
melody. Of entirely German Christmas songs, only "O Christmas Tree"
is better known. This great chorale, adapted by Bach for his 1734
"Christmas Oratorio," has been dubbed "the carol of the Reformation."

FROM HEAVEN ABOVE TO EARTH I COME

MARTIN LUTHER, 1539
Translated by CATHERINE WINKWORTH, 1855
Harmonized by J.S. BACH, 1734

© Hallmark Cards, Inc.

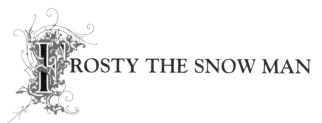ROSTY THE SNOW MAN

"Frosty The Snow Man," written by lyricist Walter E. ("Jack") Rollins
and Steve Nelson in 1950, was sort of an imaginative echo of "Rudolph
The Red-Nosed Reindeer" which appeared the year before. Both songs
were excellent and highly successful, and both created brand new
holiday characters which would become perennial favorites. Both,
in addition, spawned several television specials, including the 1969
cartoon classic "Frosty The Snow Man" narrated by Jimmy Durante.

FROSTY THE SNOW MAN

Words and Music by STEVE NELSON
and JACK ROLLINS

 O, TELL IT ON THE MOUNTAIN

This exuberant Black spiritual, created late in the 19th century or very early in the 20th century, is one of the very finest carols ever conceived. It is probably anonymous, but may possibly have been the work of Frederick J. Work, a Black Nashville-born composer.

GO, TELL IT ON THE MOUNTAIN

Black Spiritual,
ca. 1900

From the Hallmark Historical Collection.

GOD REST YE MERRY, GENTLEMEN

In Charles Dickens' 1843 Christmas classic, Scrooge chased away
a young London caroler who was singing "God Rest Ye Merry,
Gentlemen." Therefore, this song is the Christmas carol of "A
Christmas Carol." From the 16th century, it quite possibly originated
with the Waits of London, a city supported band. Despite the word
"merry" in the title and the lively, exotic melody, this superb
composition is a religious piece.

GOD REST YE MERRY, GENTLEMEN

English Folk Carol,
16th century

From the Hallmark Historical Collection. Reproduced from an original 19th century card
published by Joseph Mansell, London.

From the Hallmark Historical Collection. From an original nineteenth century card published by Louis Prang & Co., Boston.

GOOD CHRISTIAN MEN, REJOICE

In the 14th century, the carol "In Dulci Jubilo" was created. Legend says that the German Dominican mystic Heinrich Suso wrote down the song after dancing and singing with angels. In 1853, Englishman John Mason Neale freely paraphrased the medieval song, coming up with a new carol, "Good Christian Men, Rejoice," again using the old tune.

GOOD CHRISTIAN MEN, REJOICE

German, 14th century
Words translated by JOHN M. NEALE

day! _____ Christ   is   was   born   to - for   day! this!
this! _____ Christ   was   born   for   this!

HARK! THE HERALD ANGELS SING

Two giants produced this great carol. Englishman Charles Wesley, co-founder of Methodism and perhaps the top hymn writer in the English language, wrote the words in 1739. Note how the verses are saturated with theology. Almost every line is a sermon. German classical master Felix Mendelssohn composed the melody for an 1840 choral work. Different from most carols, the tune is actually a military style march!

HARK! THE HERALD ANGELS SING

Words by CHARLES WESLEY, 1739
Music by FELIX MENDELSSOHN, 1840

Joyfully

Hark! The her-ald

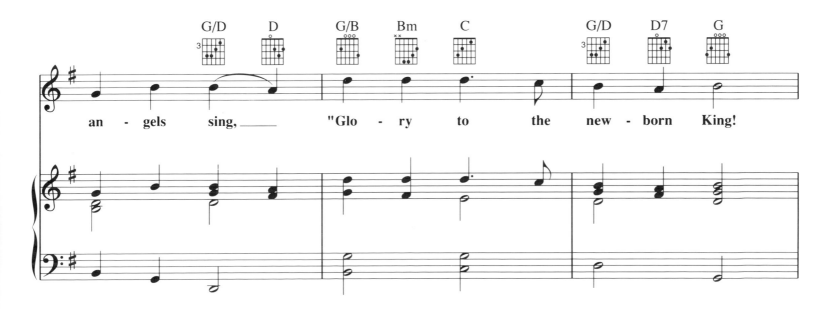

an-gels sing,_____ "Glo-ry to the new-born King!

Peace on earth, and mer - cy mild, _____ God and sin - ners re - con - ciled." Joy - ful all ye na - tions rise, _____ Join the tri - umph of the skies; _____ With th' an - gel - ic host pro - claim, "Christ is _____ born in

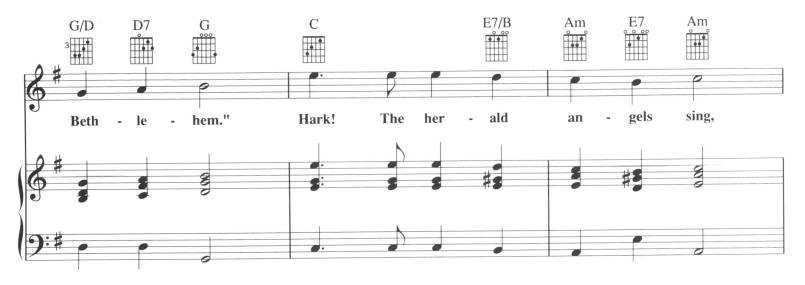

Beth - le - hem." Hark! The her - ald an - gels sing,

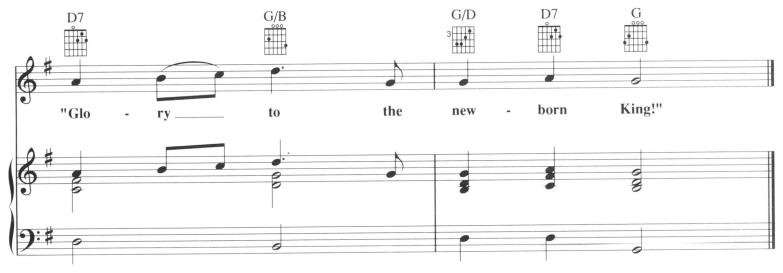

"Glo - ry _____ to the new - born King!"

ERE WE COME A-WASSAILING

This jovial, delightful 17th century folk jewel comes from Yorkshire in England. It's also known as "Wassail Song" and "Here We Come A-Caroling." The wassail is a drinking custom in which carolers go from door to door singing songs of the season and getting in return something to warm their insides.

HERE WE COME A-WASSAILING

Yorkshire Folk Carol
17th century

joy come to you, and to you your was - sail too; And God

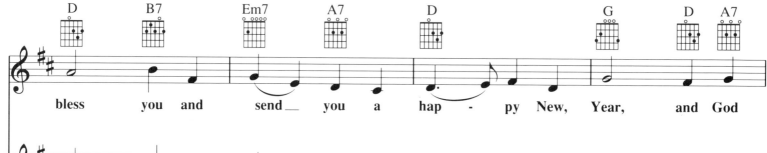

bless you and send _____ you a hap - py New, Year, and God

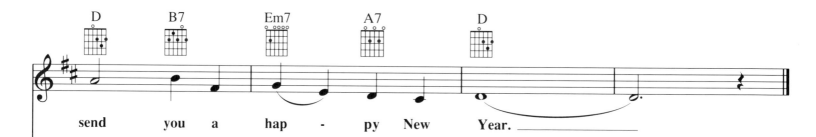

send you a hap - py New Year. _____

Additional Lyrics

3. We have got a little purse
   Of stretching leather skin;
   We want a little money
   To line it well within:

4. God bless the master of this house,
   Likewise the mistress too;
   And all the little children
   That round the table go:

From the Hallmark Historical Collection. *This is a reproduction of a design by Emily J. Harding, originally published in c.1880 by Raphael Tuck and Sons of London.*

THE HOLLY AND THE IVY

Accompanying one of the most attractive and buoyant of carol melodies is perhaps the least understood set of carol lyrics. The holly and the ivy are medieval symbols of the rivalry between the sexes, with the holly representing males and the ivy females. This celestial folk mini-masterpiece was conjured up in England around 1700.

THE HOLLY AND THE IVY

English Folk Carol, ca. 1700

all the trees that are in the wood, The____ hol - ly bears the crown. The rising of the sun____ And the run - ning of the deer, The____

Additional Lyrics

2. The holly bears a blossom,
   As white as lily flow'r,
   And Mary bore sweet Jesus Christ,
   To be our Saviour.

3. The holly bears a berry,
   As red as any blood,
   And Mary bore sweet Jesus Christ,
   To do poor sinners good.

I HEARD THE BELLS ON CHRISTMAS DAY

As much an anti-war poem as a Christmas piece, the 1863 verses by the famous American poet Henry Wadsworth Longfellow were a reaction to the wounding of his son Charley in the Civil War. The lilting, uplifting, bell-like melody was composed in 1872 by minor English composer John Baptiste Calkin.

I HEARD THE BELLS ON CHRISTMAS DAY

Words by HENRY LONGFELLOW
Adapted by JOHNNY MARKS
Music by JOHNNY MARKS

I SAW MOMMY KISSING SANTA CLAUS

Was it really Daddy in the Santa Claus suit, or was there a holiday
soap opera love triangle in the making? Only Mommy, the man
dressed as Santa, and Tommy Connor, who created this perennial
American novelty in 1952, know for sure. Jimmy Boyd's charming
recording, with a proper dose of naiveté, was largely responsible for
the song's success.

I SAW MOMMY KISSING SANTA CLAUS

Words and Music by
TOMMIE CONNOR

creep down the stairs to have a peep, she thought that I was tucked up in my bed-room fast a-sleep. Then I saw Mom-my tick-le San-ta Claus, un-der-neath his

 **'LL BE HOME FOR CHRISTMAS**

Written by lyricist James Kimball ("Kim") Gannon and composer Walter Kent in 1943, this sentimental ballad reflected the thoughts of those away from loved ones during the holiday. Since it was created at the midpoint of American participation in World War II, it was especially meaningful to men and women participating in the big conflict.

I'LL BE HOME FOR CHRISTMAS

Words and Music by KIM GANNON
and WALTER KENT

Moderately slow

I'm dream-ing to-night of a

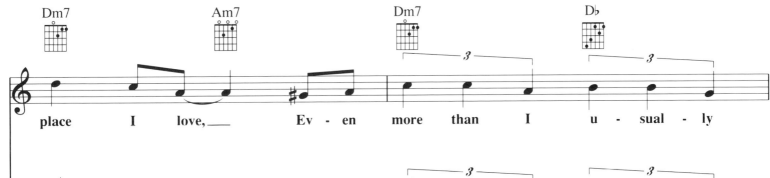

place I love,___ Ev-en more than I u-sual-ly

Where   the   love-   light   gleams,   I'll   be   home   for   Christ-   mas,   If   on-   ly   in   my

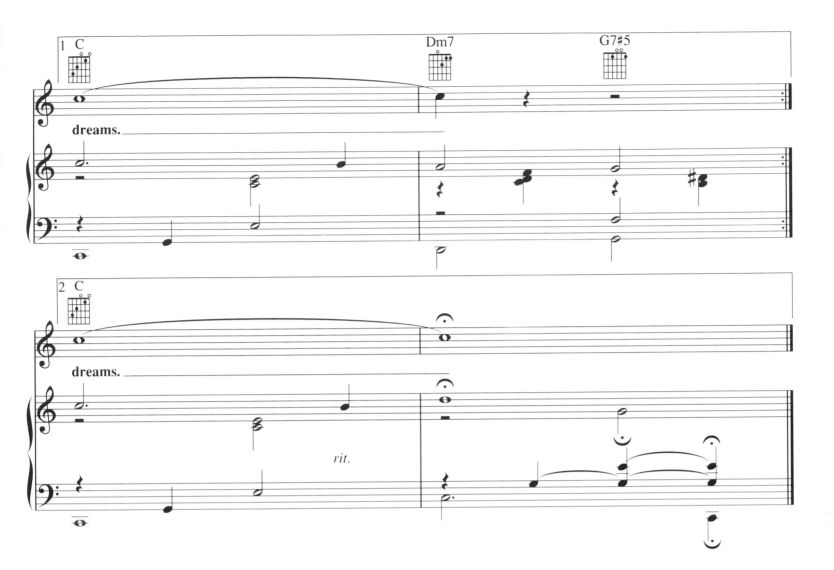

From the Hallmark Historical Collection.

IT CAME UPON THE MIDNIGHT CLEAR

Massachusetts minister Edmund Hamilton Sears created this classic poem of optimism in a wintry setting in December 1849. Boston born journalist and musician Richard Storrs Willis composed the excellent, flowing melody in 1850. Soon after, some unknown person (perhaps Willis) combined verses and melody to synthesize the first world class American carol.

IT CAME UPON THE MIDNIGHT CLEAR

Words by EDMUND H. SEARS, 1849
Music by RICHARD S. WILLIS, 1850

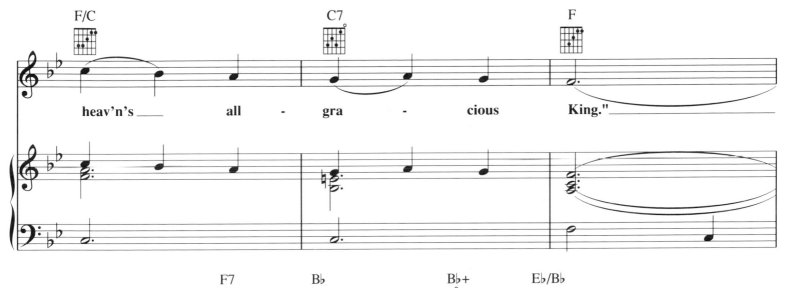

heav'n's _____ all - gra - cious King." _____

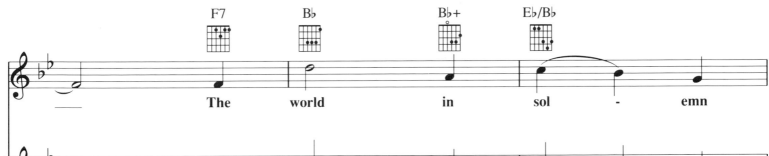

The world in sol - emn

still - ness lay, To hear the

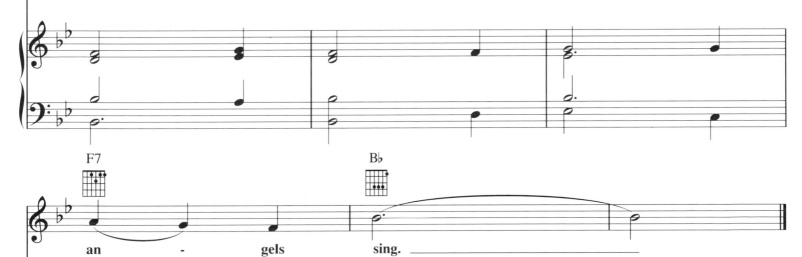

an - gels sing. _____

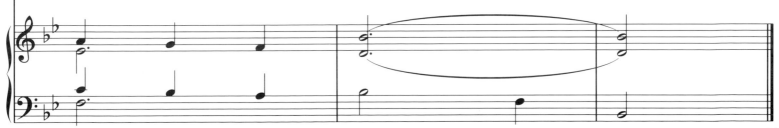

From the Hallmark Historical Collection. This is a reproduction of a postcard printed in Germany, c.1914. *Postcards were a popular form of greeting during that era and were often collected and preserved in albums.*

JINGLE BELLS

When Boston-born James S. Pierpont devised this little ditty for a Sunday school class in 1857, he surely had no idea he was creating America's first outstanding secular Christmas song and probably its most popular. Incidentally, "Jingle Bell Rock," the best Christmas rock song, was written by Joseph Beal and James Boothe exactly one hundred years later, in 1957.

JINGLE BELLS

Words and Music by
J. PIERPONT

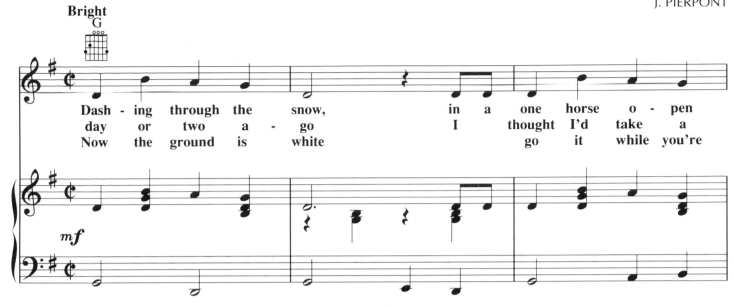

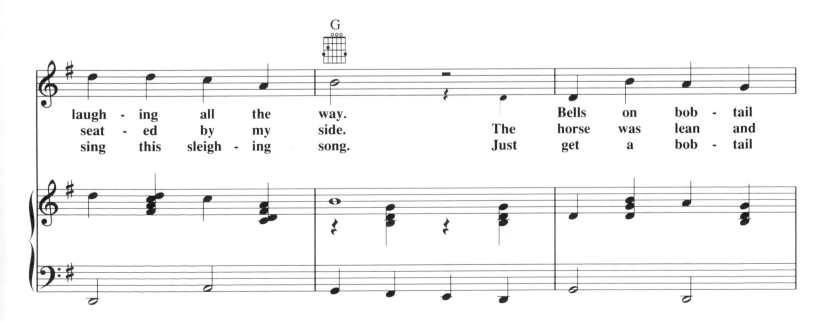

From the Hallmark Historical Collection. *Reproduced from an original 1886 card published by Louis Prang, Boston, designed by Walter Satterlee.*

JOLLY OLD ST. NICHOLAS

This bright and lively American holiday favorite, quite popular among children, is anonymous. It was probably written in the second half of the 19th century or very early in the 20th. There is a chance it was composed by Benjamin R. Hanby, who created the similar style "Up On The Housetop" in the 1850's or 1860's.

JOLLY OLD ST. NICHOLAS

From the Hallmark Historical Collection. Reproduced from an original 19th century card
published by Charles Goodall & Son, London.

JOY TO THE WORLD

The verses for this spectacular carol were penned in 1719 by Englishman
Isaac Watts, whose English language hymn writing accomplishments are
only challenged by Charles Wesley. In 1839, the lyrics were published
with a sweeping, dynamic melody accompanied by a notation attributing
the music to German master George Frederick Handel. But the real
composer of the tune was American hymnist Lowell Mason who first
published it.

JOY TO THE WORLD

ISAAC WATTS, 1719,
LOWELL MASON, 1839

ET IT SNOW! LET IT SNOW! LET IT SNOW!

Although not at all mentioning the holiday season, this charming 1945 novelty by wordsmith Sammy Cahn and tunesmith Jule Styne has become a perennial favorite at Christmastime. It's perhaps the only time a song has encouraged a snowstorm, thus giving romantic couples an excuse to stay inside.

LET IT SNOW! LET IT SNOW! LET IT SNOW!

Words by SAMMY CAHN
Music by JULE STYNE

finally kiss good-night, How I'll hate go-ing out in the storm! But if you'll real-ly hold me tight, All the way home I'll be warm. The snow!

O, HOW A ROSE E'ER BLOOMING

The rose referred to here is Mary, the mother of Jesus. One of the finest songs of the 15th century, this exquisite piece survived the religious hostilities of the 16th century Lutheran reformers. The carol has been sometimes attributed to Michael Praetorius, who arranged and popularized the tune.

LO, HOW A ROSE E'ER BLOOMING

German Folk Carol, 15th century
Translated by THEODORE BAKER, 1894
Harmonization by MICHAEL PRAETORIUS, 1609

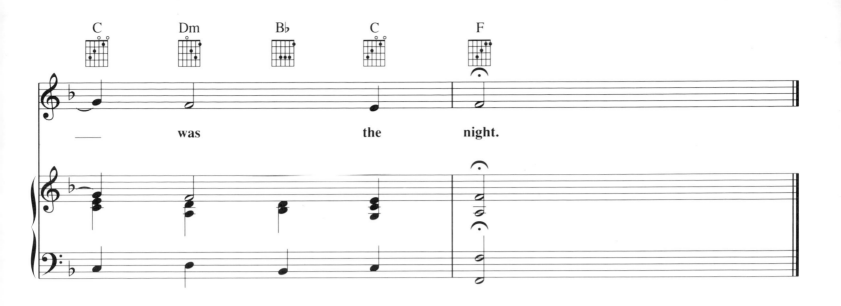

was   the   night.

Additional Lyrics

2. Isaiah 'twas foretold it,
   The Rose I have in mind,
   With Mary we behold it,
   The Virgin Mother kind.
   To show God's love aright,
   She bore to men a Savior
   When half-spent was the night.

3. This Flow'r, whose fragrance tender
   With sweetness fills the air,
   Dispels with glorious splendor
   The darkness ev'rywhere.
   True man, yet very God;
   From sin and death He saves us,
   And lightens ev'ry load.

MARCH OF THE TOYS

The most beloved stage production by renowned Irish-American composer Victor Herbert was "Babes In Toyland" (1903). From that operetta came this spritely little march inspiring the gallant rescue efforts of a batch of Christmas toys.

MARCH OF THE TOYS

By VICTOR HERBERT, 1903

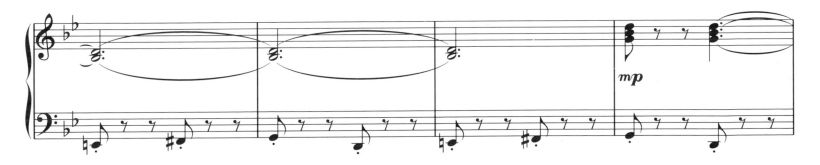

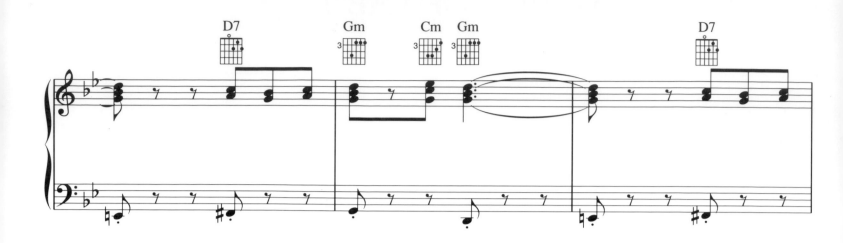

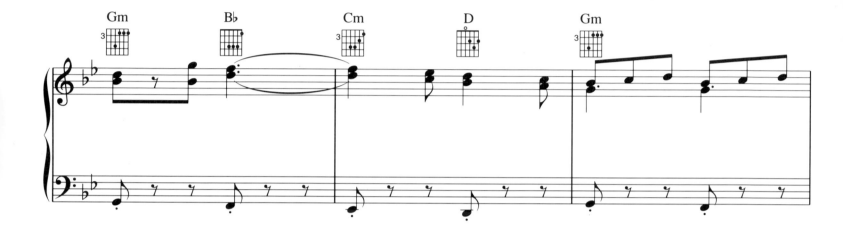

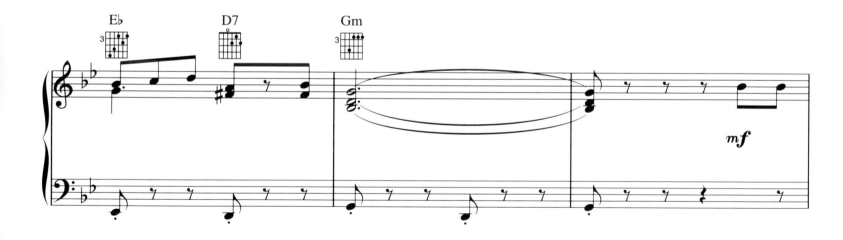

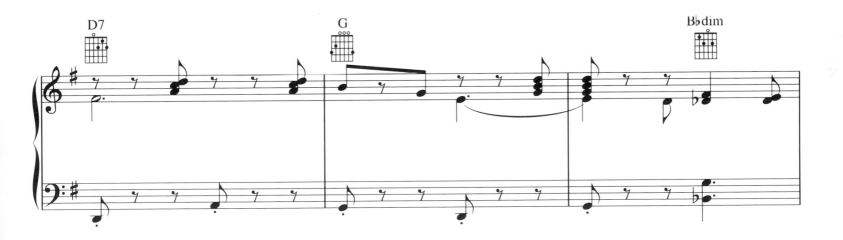

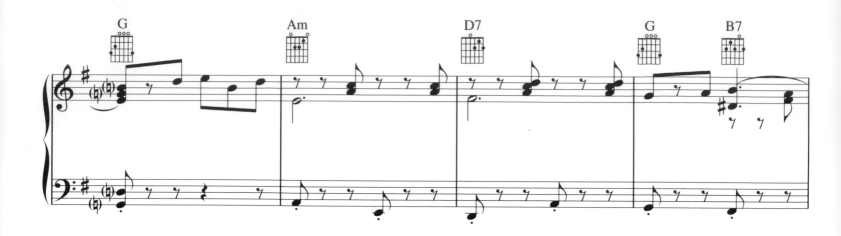

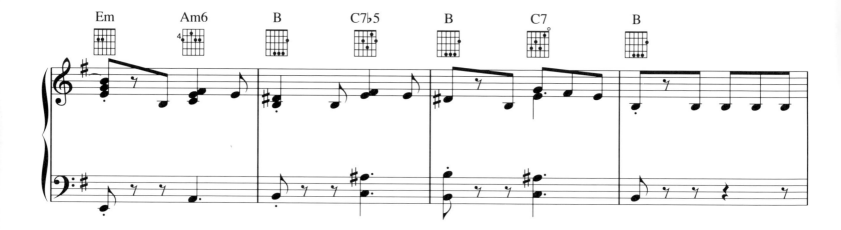

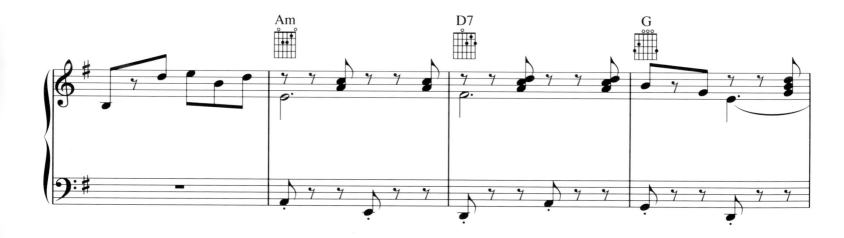

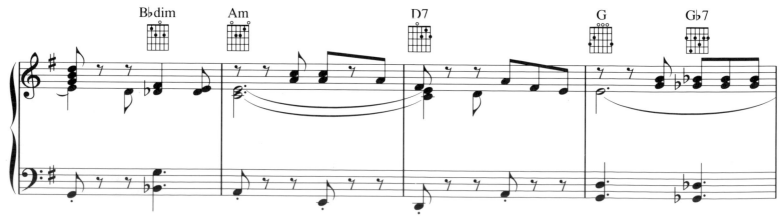

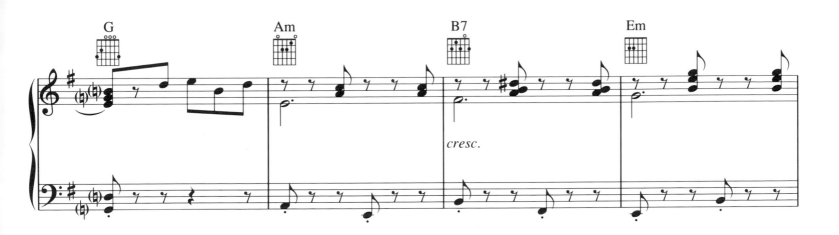

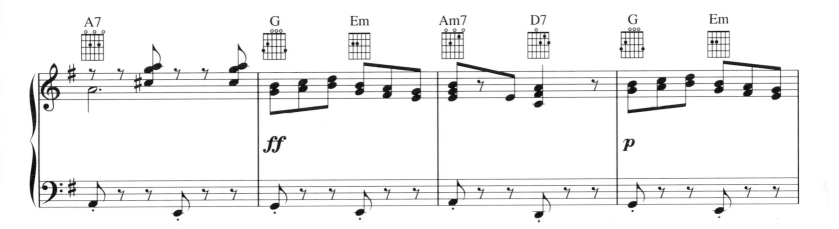

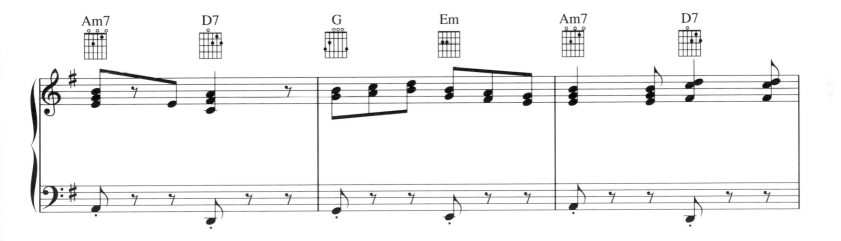

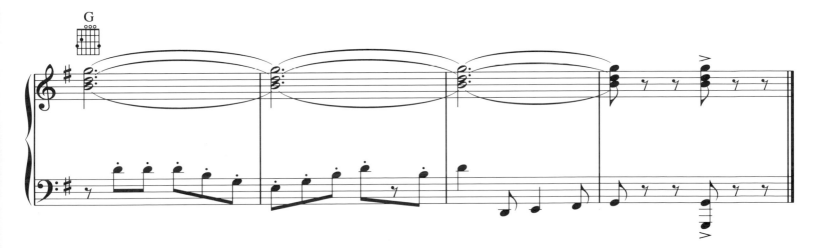

MARY HAD A BABY

The fragile image of the blessed young woman Mary with her helpless
infant Christ child was a popular theme in Black-American carols.
This piece, among the best of its type, was probably created in the
19th century, possibly in South Carolina.

MARY HAD A BABY

Black Spiritual
probably 19th century

1. Mar - y had a ba - by,
3. She called Him Je - sus
5. - 7. *(See additional lyrics)*

Oh Lord;__ Mar - y had a ba - by, Oh my__ Lord;
Oh Lord;__ She called Him Je - sus Oh my__ Lord;

Mar - y had a ba - by, Oh Lord;__ { The peo - ple keep a - com - ing and the
She called Him Je - sus, Oh Lord;__ {

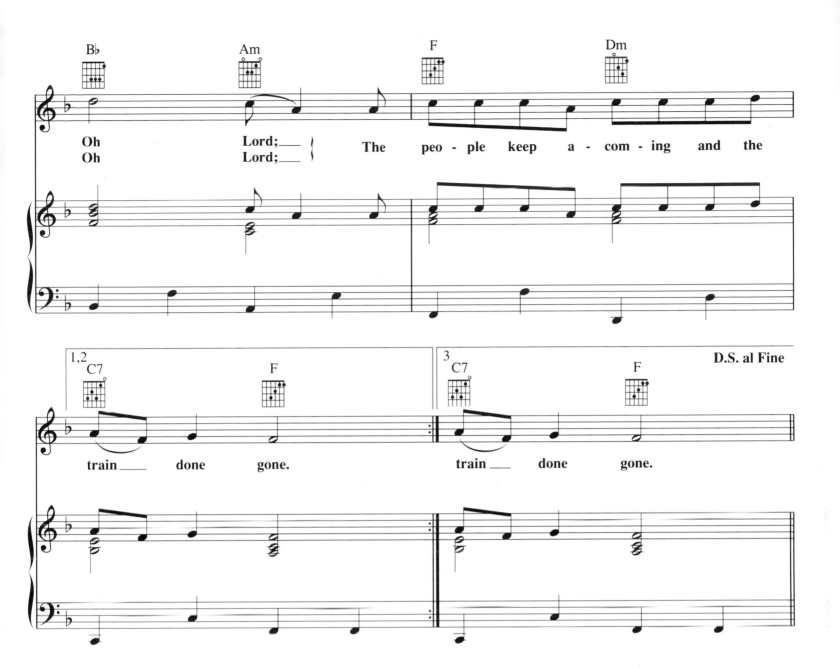

Additional Lyrics

5. Born in a stable, Oh Lord;
   Born in a stable, Oh my Lord;
   Born in a stable, Oh Lord;
   The people keep a-coming and the train done gone.

6. Where did they lay Him? Oh Lord;
   Where did they lay Him? Oh my Lord;
   Where did they lay Him? Oh Lord;
   The people keep a-coming and the train done gone.

7. Laid Him in a manger, Oh Lord;
   Laid Him in a manger, Oh my Lord;
   Laid Him in a manger, Oh Lord;
   The people keep a-coming and the train done gone.

CHRISTMAS TREE

It has sometimes been thought that this German folk carol originated in the Middle Ages. Yet the style of the music plus the fact that Christmas trees were not a popular holiday institution until the 16th century suggest that the song was created around the 16th or 17th centuries. The melody is excellent, but the German words and all English translations seem awkward.

O CHRISTMAS TREE

German

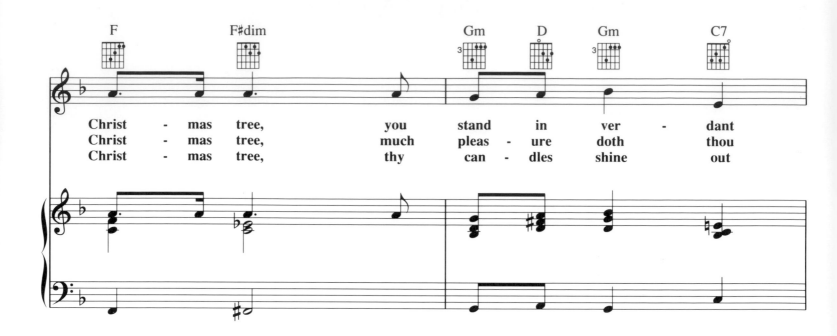

Christ - mas tree, you stand in ver - dant
Christ - mas tree, much stand pleas - ure doth thou
Christ - mas tree, thy can - dles shine out

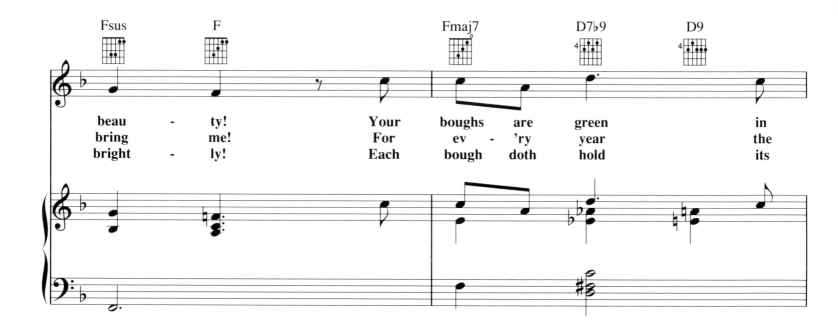

beau - ty! Your boughs are green in
bring me! For ev - 'ry year the
bright - ly! Each bough doth hold its

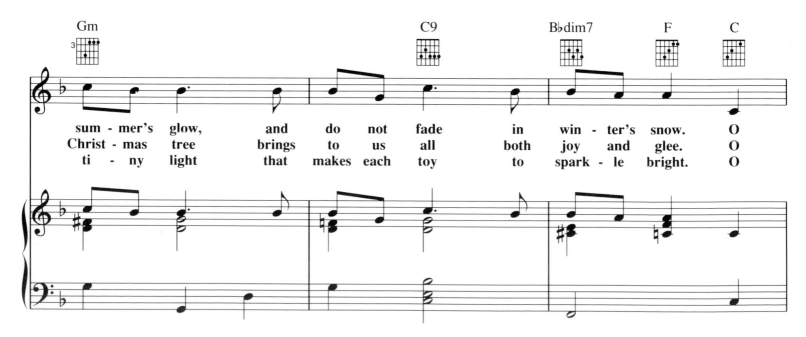

sum - mer's glow, and do not fade in win - ter's snow. O
Christ - mas tree brings to us all both joy and glee. O
ti - ny light that makes each toy to spark - le bright. O

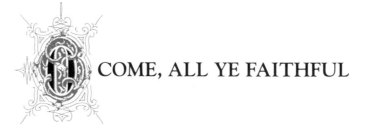 COME, ALL YE FAITHFUL

Catholic Englishman John Francis Wade, a music teacher and music copyist, wrote this magnificent Latin carol between 1740 and 1743 while living in Douai, France. For two centuries, English, German, Italian, and Portuguese origins were claimed. Because of this background and the song's great world-wide acceptance, it deserves the epithet of "the international carol."

O COME, ALL YE FAITHFUL

JOHN FRANCIS WADE, between 1740 and 1743;
Translated by FREDERICH OAKELEY, 1852

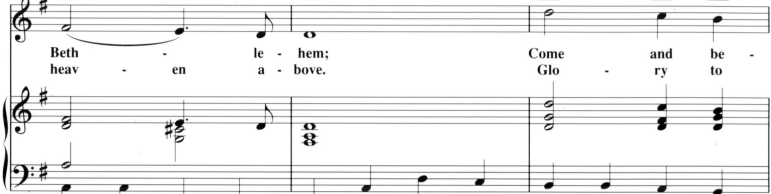

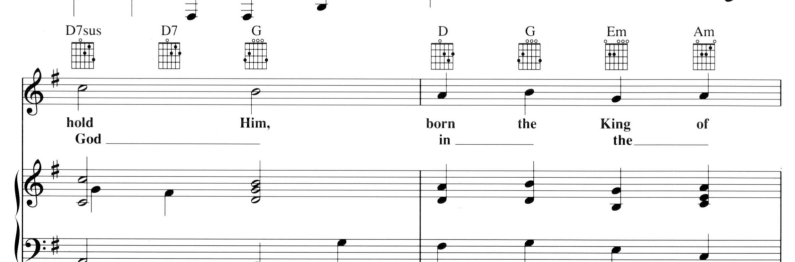

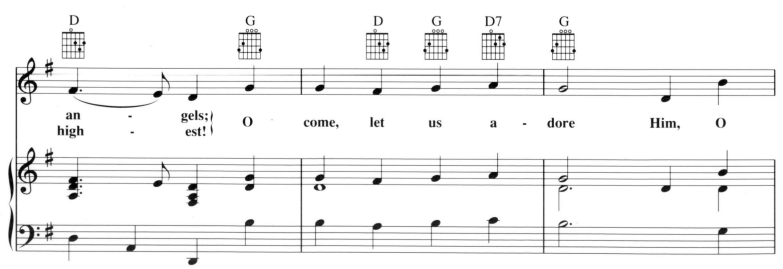

148

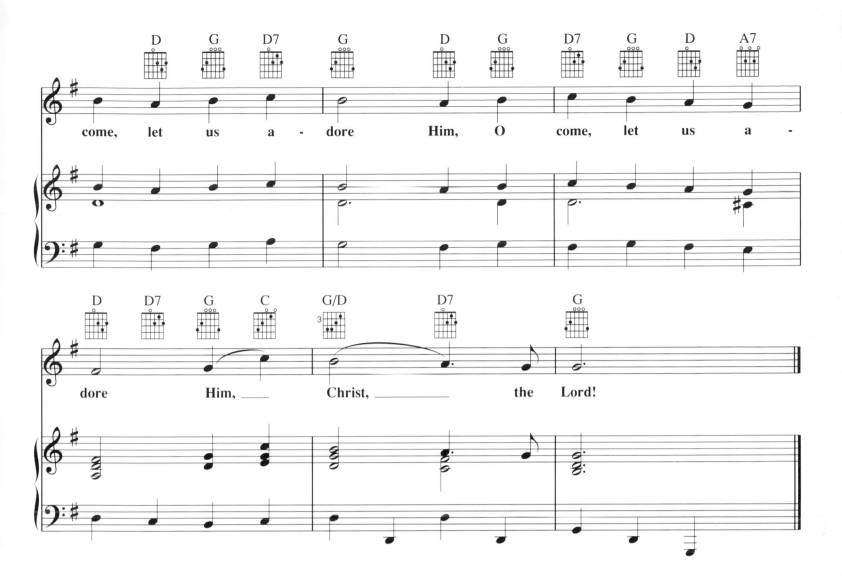

come, let us a - dore Him, O come, let us a -

dore Him, _____ Christ, _____ the Lord!

 COME, LITTLE CHILDREN

Many carols have been created for children, but few have been specifically written about children. Christoph von Schmid, a German Catholic priest and schoolmaster, penned the words around 1850. Johann Abraham Peter Schulz, a German composer, conductor, and organist, wrote the melody around 1790 while living in Denmark.

O COME, LITTLE CHILDREN

CHRISTOPH von SCHMID, ca. 1850
JOHANN ABRAHAM PETER SCHULZ, ca. 1790

O come, lit-tle chil-dren, from cot and from hall, O come to the man-ger in Beth-le-hem's stall. There

meek - ly He li - eth, the heav - en - ly
Child, So poor and so hum - ble, so
sweet and so mild. Now "Glo - ry to
God!" sing the an - gels on high, And

"Peace up - on earth!" heav'n - ly voic - es re -

ply. Then come lit - tle chil - dren, and

join in the day That glad - dened the

world on that first Christ - mas Day.

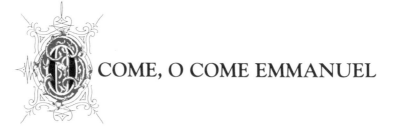 COME, O COME EMMANUEL

This soulful Advent carol could be called "a carol of two centuries."
Both its original Latin lyrics and its melody (supposedly a plainsong
or chant) are said, without proof, to be from about the 12th century.
But it was not assembled as a carol until 1854 when two Englishmen,
Thomas Helmore and John Mason Neale, published it. Reportedly,
Helmore adapted the old music and Neale translated the words (with
later modifications by Henry S. Coffin).

O COME, O COME EMMANUEL

Translated by JOHN M. NEALE
and HENRY S. COFFIN
Possibly 12th century

Like an old plainsong

O

Come, O Come Em - man - u - el, And

ran - som cap - tive Is - ra - el, That

mourns in lone - ly ex - ile here Un -

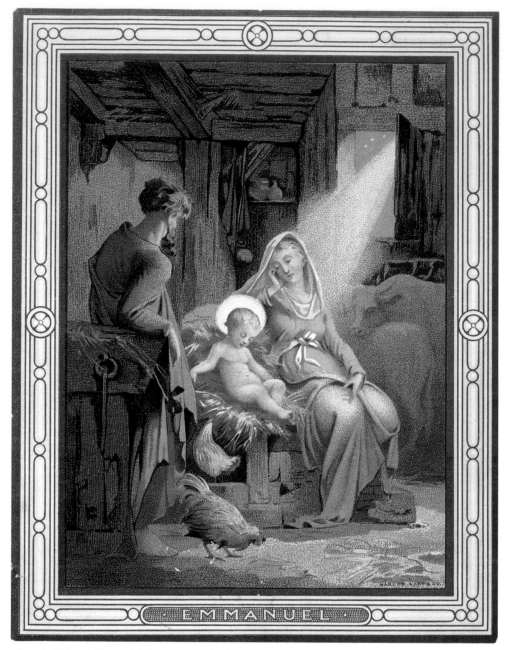

From the Hallmark Historical Collection. *Reproduced from an original 19th century card published by Marcus Ward & Co., London.*

 HOLY NIGHT

In December 1847, Placide Cappeau, a commissionaire of wines and part-time poet from southern France, travelled to Paris to visit the celebrated classical composer Adolphe Adam. The musician consented to write a melody to go with Cappeau's just completed Christmas poem. The resultant carol, the greatest Christmas song from France, premiered that year at Cappeau's home church.

O HOLY NIGHT

English Words by J.S. DWIGHT
Music by ADOLPHE ADAM

 LITTLE TOWN OF BETHLEHEM

In December 1868, Philadelphia clergyman Phillips Brooks penned
some verses reminiscing on a trip to the Holy Land a few years earlier.
His friend Lewis H. Redner, a real estate broker and part-time organist,
was asked to supply a musical setting for an upcoming Sunday school
program. Redner reportedly went to bed the night before the program
and woke up with "an angel strain" sounding in his head. He jotted
down some notes and a classic was born.

O LITTLE TOWN OF BETHLEHEM

Words by PHILLIPS BROOKS, 1868
Music by LEWIS H. REDNER, 1868

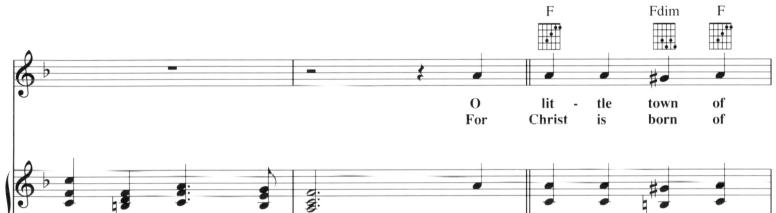

O lit - tle town of
For Christ is born of

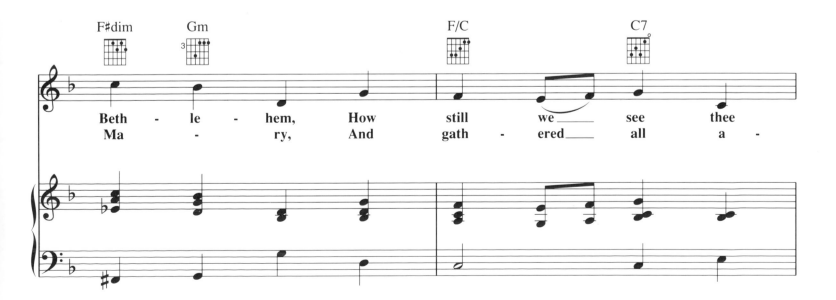

Beth - le - hem, How still we see thee
Ma - ry, And gath - ered all a -

light;   The   hopes   and   fears   of
birth!   And   prais   -   es   sing   to

all   the   years   Are   met   in   thee   to - night.
God   the   King,   And   peace   to   men   on   earth!

ONCE IN ROYAL DAVID'S CITY

Many carols have interesting histories, but this one doesn't. The only thing unusual about this song is that the lyrics were written by a woman named Cecil. A female English hymn writer, Cecil Frances Alexander, penned the lines in 1848. An otherwise undistinguished English organist and composer, Henry J. Gauntlett, created the tune in 1849.

ONCE IN ROYAL DAVID'S CITY

CECIL FRANCES ALEXANDER, 1848
HENRY J. GAUNTLETT, 1849

for __ His __ bed. Ma - ry was that moth - er mild,

Je - sus Christ her lit - tle__ Child. And our eyes at

last __ shall __ see Him, Through His own re - deem - ing__ love,

For that Child so dear__ and__ gen - tle Is our Lord in

heav'n a - bove. And He leads His child - ren on

To the place where He is gone.

RISE UP, SHEPHERD, AND FOLLOW

Published in 1867, this excellent Black spiritual probably dates from the late 18th or early 19th century. Frequently, a solo voice sings the verses followed by a vocal ensemble responding with the key phrase, "Rise up, shepherd, and follow."

RISE UP, SHEPHERD, AND FOLLOW

Black Spiritual

RUDOLPH THE RED-NOSED REINDEER

The original story of Rudolph was created by Robert L. May in 1939 as part of an advertising promotion. Ten years later, in 1949, May's brother-in-law Johnny Marks wrote this phenomenally successful novelty. Among 20th century holiday songs, only "White Christmas" has surpassed the public acceptance of "Rudolph." Several television specials starring the reindeer have appeared, most notably the 1964 classic narrated by "Snowman" Burl Ives.

RUDOLPH THE RED-NOSED REINDEER

Music and Lyrics by
JOHNNY MARKS

call the most fa - mous rein-deer of all.

Ru - dolph, the red - nosed rein - deer had a ver - y shin - y

a tempo

nose, and if you ev - er saw it,

you would e - ven say it glows. All of the oth - er

rein - deer used to laugh and call him

C/E   E♭dim

names, they nev - er let poor

G7

Ru - dolph join in an - y rein - deer

games. Then one fog - gy Christ - mas Eve,

C   C7   F   C   C7

SILENT NIGHT

Except for a series of accidents, the greatest of carols would not have
been created. Because the organ at the church in Oberndorf, Austria
had become unplayable because of rust in 1818, Father Joseph Mohr
wrote a simple set of lyrics and organist Franz Grüber created a simple
melody to use in the Christmas Eve service. Mohr, a problem priest
who was frequently transferred, was not at Oberndorf long. And
Gruber was supposed to be at another church. Furthermore, the song
would have died there if it were not for the organ repairman who
obtained a copy and began its spread around the world.

SILENT NIGHT

Words by JOSEPH MOHR
Music by FRANZ GRÜBER

Quietly

Si - lent night, ho - ly night!
Si - lent night, ho - ly night!
Si - lent night, ho - ly night!

All is calm, all is bright.
Shep - herds quake at the sight.
Son of God love's pure light.

Round yon Vir - gin Moth - er and Child.
Glo - ries stream from heav - en a far,
Ra - diant beams from Thy ho - ly face

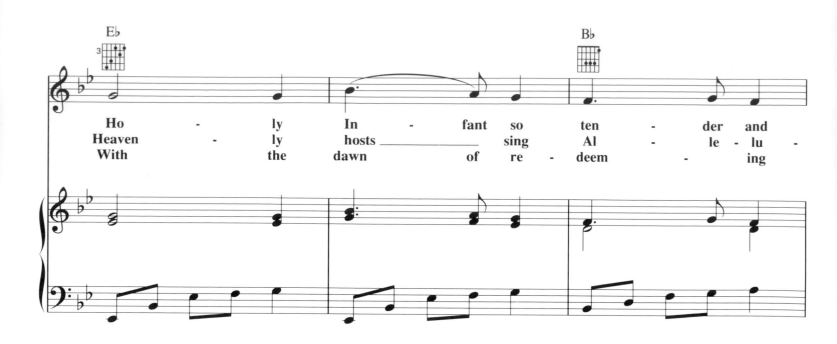

Ho - ly In - fant so ten - der and
Heaven - ly hosts _____ sing Al - le - lu -
With the dawn of re - deem - ing

mild, Sleep in heav - en - ly
ia, Christ the Sav - ior is
grace, Je - sus, Lord, at Thy

peace, _____ Sleep _____ in
born! _____ Christ _____ the
birth. _____ Je - sus

184

F7   Bb

heav - en - ly   peace.
Sav - ior is   born!
Lord   at Thy   birth.

185

SING WE NOW OF CHRISTMAS

The Provence region of southern France has produced several outstanding folk carols. "The March Of The Kings," a lively 13th century marvel, "Bring A Torch, Jeannette, Isabella," a brilliant 17th century jewel, and "Sing We Now Of Christmas," a joyful 17th or 18th century piece, all originated in that hotbed of Christmas music.

SING WE NOW OF CHRISTMAS

Provence Folk Carol;
17th or 18th century

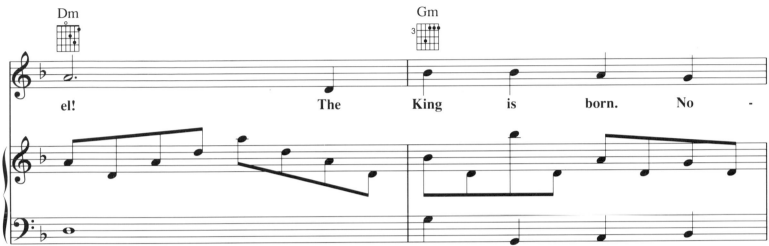

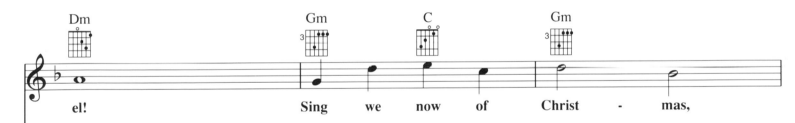

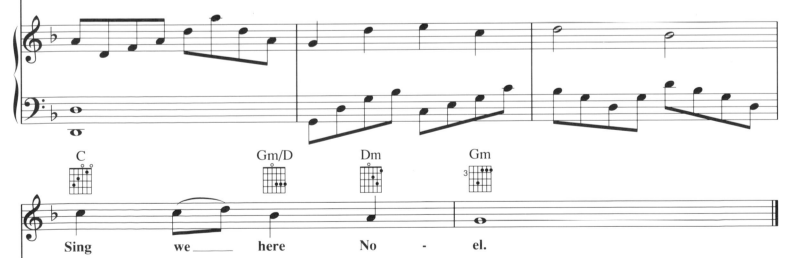

STILL, STILL, STILL

Salzburg, Austria pops up frequently in the history of music. The incomparable master Wolfgang Amadeus Mozart was born there. The Von Trapp family singers of "The Sound Of Music" won a music festival there. And two carols, "Silent Night" and the 18th or 19th century folk lullaby "Still, Still, Still," were created in the region.

STILL, STILL, STILL

Austrian Folk Carol,
18th or 19th century

TOYLAND

The fanciful "little girl and boy land" described by Brooklyn-born Glen MacDonough in this ballad will continue long after this song is forgotten. Lovingly carried by a gentle waltz by the famous Irish-American composer Victor Herbert, "Toyland" was the hit of the 1903 operetta "Babes In Toyland."

TOYLAND

Words by GLEN MAC DONOUGH
Music by VICTOR HERBERT

 HE TWELVE DAYS OF CHRISTMAS

With an accessible melody and clever counting lyrics, this 17th or 18th century English folk phenomenon is always a big hit at Christmas. It's a song conducive to tinkering and variation, and a song with a most charming personality. The concept for the composition may have come from France, where a similar piece exists.

THE TWELVE DAYS OF CHRISTMAS

English Folk Song,
17th or 18th century

On the first day of Christ-mas, my
true love gave to me: A par-tridge in a pear tree.

2. On the
3. On the
4. On the

sec-ond day of Christ-mas, my true love sent to me:
third day of Christ-mas, my true love sent to me:
fourth day of Christ-mas, my true love sent to me:

Repeat as needed

C7

Two tur - tle doves,
Three French __ hens,
Four call - ing birds,

And a par - tridge __ in a pear

F   Bb   F   C7

D.S. for verses 3-4

F   Bb   F

tree.

On the fifth day of Christ - mas, my

C7   F   G7   C

true love sent to me: Five gold _____ rings.

F   Gm   C7

Four __ call - ing birds, Three French hens, Two __ tur - tle doves, And a

199

UP ON THE HOUSETOP

Little known Ohioan Benjamin R. Hanby wrote this children's favorite sometime in the 1850s or 1860s. It is possible that Hanby also created "Jolly Old St. Nicholas," an anonymous holiday song with similar style lyrics and music.

UP ON THE HOUSETOP

By BENJAMIN R. HANBY

Brightly

Up on the house - top ___ rein - deer pause,
First comes the stock - ing of lit - tle Nell;

Out jumps good old San - ta Claus;
Oh, dear good San - ta, fill it well;

Down thru the chim - ney with lots of toys,
Give her a dol - lie that laughs and cries,

Down thru the chim - ney with good Saint Nick.

 VIRGIN MOST PURE

From the old-fashioned title one would think this English song is from the Middle Ages. Yet most likely, the folk lyrics date from the 17th century and the folk tune dates from the 18th. Considering that sophisticated carols like "The Holly And The Ivy" and "The Twelve Days Of Christmas" date from about the same time, this piece seems chronologically out of place.

A VIRGIN MOST PURE

English Folk Carol, 17th century
English Folk Tune, 18th century

be our Re - deem - er from death hell ____ and sin, which ____ A - dam's trans - gres - sion hath ____ wrapped ____ us in. And ____

Additional Lyrics

2. At Bethlem in Jewry a city there was
   Where Joseph and Mary together did pass,
   All for to be taxed with many one moe.
   For Caesar commanded the same should be so.

3. But when they had entered the city so fair,
   A number of people so mighty was there,
   That Joseph and Mary, whose substance was small,
   Could find in the inn there no lodging at all.

4. Then were they constrained in a stable to lie,
   Where horses and asses they used for to tie;
   Their lodging so simple they took it no scorn,
   But against the next morning our Saviour was born.

5. The King of all kings to this world being brought,
   Small store of fine linen to wrap Him was sought,
   But when she had swaddled her young Son so sweet,
   Within an ox-manger she laid Him to sleep.

6. Then God sent an angel from heaven so high
   To certain poor shepherds in fields where they lie,
   And bade them no longer in sorrow to stay,
   Because that our Saviour was born on this day.

7. Then presently after the shepherds did spy
   Vast numbers of angels to stand in the sky;
   They joyfully talked and sweetly did sing:
   "To God be all glory, our heavenly King."

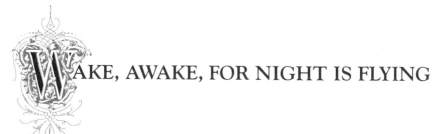AKE, AWAKE, FOR NIGHT IS FLYING

Not everyone writes pieces like the "King of chorales" ("Wake, Awake, for the Night is Flying") and the "Queen of chorales" ("O Morning Star, How Fair and Bright") in the same year (1599). Yet Philipp Nicolai, a well-known German minister, managed to compose a pair of little royal masterpieces in the midst of an epidemic of bubonic plague.

WAKE, AWAKE, FOR NIGHT IS FLYING

PHILIPP NICOLAI, 1599
Harmonized by J.S. BACH

Additional Lyrics

2. Zion hears the watchmen singing,
   Her heart with deep delight is springing,
   She wakes, she rises from her gloom:
   Forth her Bridegroom comes, all glorious,
   In grace arrayed, by truth victorious;
   Her Star is risen, her Light is come!
   All hail, Incarnate Lord,
   Our crown, and our reward!
   Alleluia!
   We haste along, in pomp of song,
   And gladsome join the marriage throng.

3. Lamb of God, the heav'ns adore Thee,
   And men and angels sing before Thee,
   With harp and cymbal's clearest tone.
   By the pearly gates in wonder
   We stand, and swell the voice of thunder
   That echoes round Thy dazzling throne.
   No vision ever brought,
   No ear hath ever caught,
   Such bliss and joy:
   We raise the song, we swell the throng,
   To praise Thee ages all along.

 E THREE KINGS OF ORIENT ARE

This pseudo-oriental classic, with a compelling melody and somewhat clumsy lyrics has often been regarded as an old song. But it was created in 1857, the same year that the newer-sounding "Jingle Bells" came to life. Its author was Pittsburgh-born clergyman, journalist, and artist John Henry Hopkins who offered it to his Vermont nephews and nieces as a Christmas gift.

WE THREE KINGS OF ORIENT ARE

Words and Music by
JOHN H. HOPKINS, 1857

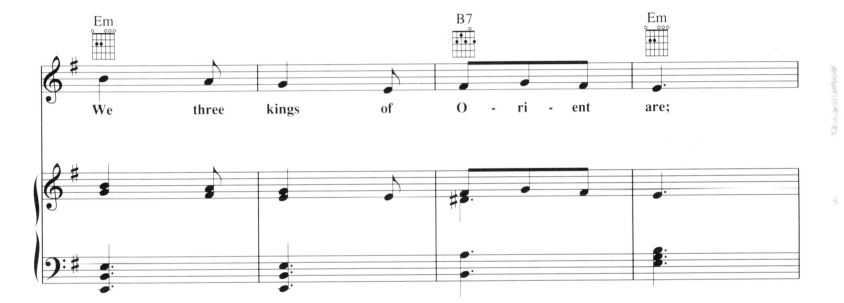

We three kings of O - ri - ent are;

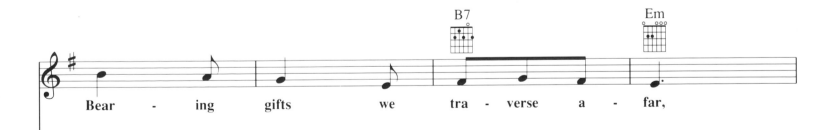

Bear - ing gifts we tra - verse a - far,

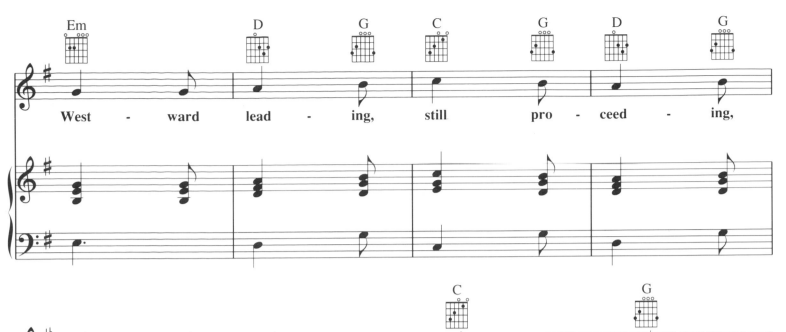

Westward lead - ing, still pro - ceed - ing,

Guide us to thy per - fect light.

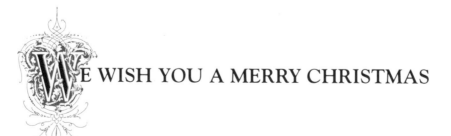

WE WISH YOU A MERRY CHRISTMAS

Although not the most brilliantly conceived composition ever, this jolly and attracting folk concoction very pleasantly continues to spread holiday greetings century after century. It was created in the West Country of England, quite possibly in the highly productive 16th century.

WE WISH YOU A MERRY CHRISTMAS

English

Brightly

mf

G

We wish you a Mer - ry Christ - mas, We

C   **E7**

A7   **D**   **B7**

wish you a Mer - ry Christ - mas, We wish you a Mer - ry

Em   **G/B**   **C**   **D7**   **G**

Christ - mas, and a hap - py New Year. Good

WHAT CHILD IS THIS?

The lyrics by English insurance executive and occasional poet
William Chatterton Dix, written around 1865, are quite good. But it
is the exquisite English folk melody, also known as "Greensleeves,"
which makes this carol exceptional. "Greensleeves," which has been
wrongly attributed to King Henry VIII, was most likely created during
the second half of the 16th century (about the time of Shakespeare
and Queen Elizabeth I).

WHAT CHILD IS THIS?

English

Slow and Serene

What Child is this, who, laid to
So bring Him in - cense, gold and

rest, On Ma - ry's lap is
myrrh, Come peas - ant king to

sleep - ing? Whom an - gels
own Him; The King of

greet _____ with an - thems sweet _____ While
kings _____ sal - va - tion brings, _____ Let

shep - herds watch _____ are keep -
lov - ing hearts _____ en - throne

ing? This,
Him. Raise,

this _____ is
raise _____ the

Christ the King, _____ Whom shep - herds
song on high, _____ The Vir - gin

PEACE